Golden Retriev Training Book: The Simple Step-By-Step Guide To Golden Retriever Puppy Training

Training includes Fetch, Sit, Stay, Potty Training, Socialization and Leash Training

All Rights Reserved worldwide. No part of this publication may be reproduced in any form or by any means, including scanning, photocopying, or otherwise without prior written permission of the copyright holder.

Copyright © 2017

Golden Retriever Training Book: How to Train Your Golden Retriever Puppy 1

   Introduction to the Golden Retriever 5

   Is the Golden Retriever a Good Choice for You?.......8

   How Does a Golden Retriever Differ from a Labrador Retriever?.. 13

   What Kinds of Exercise Do Golden Retrievers Like Best? 15

      Walking.. 18

      Hunting 19

      Playtime.. 20

   Choosing a Golden Retriever Puppy........................ 21

   What to Do After You've Brought Your Golden Retriever Puppy Home 25

   Communicating with Your Golden Retriever............ 27

   Disciplining Your Dog 31

   Potty Training Your Puppy... 33

   Basic Obedience Training... 35

   Know Your Dog 37

   Quickly Get Your Dog Accustomed to his Name..... 38

   Watch Out for Signs that Your Dog Might Not Trust You 39

How to Teach Your Golden Retriever to Sit on Command 42

How to Teach Your Golden Retriever to Drop on Command 44

How to Teach Your Golden Retriever to Come on Command (Recall) 45

How to Teach Your Golden Retriever to Fetch on Command 47

Leash Training Your Golden Retriever 53

    Selecting the Right Leash and Collar 54

    Leash Training Your Golden Retriever Puppy 55

    Next Steps in Leash Training 57

What to Do When Coming Across Strangers and Other Dogs 60

Socializing Your Golden Retriever 62

How to Address Your Dog's Chewing or Biting 64

Advanced Techniques and Agility Training 68

Conclusion 72

Introduction to the Golden Retriever

The Golden Retriever (often referred to as simply "the Golden") is one of the world's most popular breeds of dog. A friendly, affectionate, and playful pet, the Golden Retriever is especially suitable for families.

It has not only a pleasing and flexible personality but a beautiful appearance, with a long, shiny golden coat. The Golden Retriever is also a highly intelligent canine.

The Golden Retriever is outgoing and loyal, and is prized for its sweet, loving nature. While it can occasionally be a reasonably decent watch dog, it is generally a terrible choice as a guard dog because of its invariably open, friendly temperament.

Golden Retrievers are good at interacting with both humans and other dogs. The Golden Retriever is a retriever, which means that it was bred to retrieve prey (especially waterfowl) during the hunt.

It was often required to swim while doing so, and it has been bred to have many characteristics that make it perfect for the water.

The coat color of Golden Retrievers ranges from lighter to darker shades of gold. The coat is a double coat, and it can be either straight or wavy in texture. The Golden Retriever's coat needs lots of brushing, and the occasional bath will be necessary.

Regular ear cleaning is also necessary. Golden Retrievers are medium-to-large dogs, ranging from 55 to 75 pounds on average. Males usually weigh more and are larger than females.

The Golden Retriever is the fourth most intelligent breed of dog, coming after the Border Collie, Poodle, and German Shepherd. The breed's intelligence and loyalty makes it an excellent guide dog for the blind and disabled.

They are also often search and rescue dogs, tracking dogs, and obedience competitors. Golden Retrievers are known for being cooperative and easy to train, a fact that strongly contributes to its popularity.

Golden Retrievers are relatively large dogs that need space and lots of exercise in order to thrive and be happy. They are energetic and love fun and games with their human companions.

History of the Golden Retriever Breed

The Golden Retriever's heritage can be traced back to nineteenth-century Britain, when people began breeding dogs that would be useful in retrieving game (especially waterfowl) for hunters.

In 1865, a man called Dudley Marjoribanks living in the Highlands of Scotland found a yellow puppy in a litter that was otherwise black in color. He eventually had this dog, which he called "Nous", bred with a Tweed Water Spaniel (this breed no longer exists).

The puppies there were born from this, which were all yellow, became the Golden Retriever's breed foundation. After more careful breeding, the Golden Retriever was created.

It was in 1904 that the Golden Retriever became well-known. They were first referred to as "Yellow Retrievers". The breed was registered as the Golden Retriever by the American Kennel Club in 1925.

Is the Golden Retriever a Good Choice for You?

While the Golden Retriever is a great family dog, there are many factors and realities that you should think about before deciding to make the commitment of getting a Golden Retriever puppy.

One is the fact that you will need a certain amount of space for your home to be suitable for a Golden Retriever. If you have any doubt that your living space is big enough, it is better to go with a smaller breed.

Golden Retrievers need at least an hour and a half of exercise outside every day. This will likely mean that you will need a yard (a fenced one, preferably).

Golden Retriever owners must enjoy spending time in the outdoors. The Golden Retriever won't be happy unless their human companion is outside playing with them, so you will not be able to expect your dog to be content just being in the yard by itself.

Remember that Golden Retrievers are a sporting breed; they have lots of energy. If they are not able to burn off their energy, they are likely to become destructive (for example, turn to chewing your possessions). If you are not an energetic person, you would be happier with a breed with lesser exercise needs.

Remember all the costs involved in having a Golden Retriever during the course of the animal's life, which will hopefully be more than 12 years. Examples of expenses include:

- Vet bills and/or pet insurance: Vet bills can really add up, especially if your pet has health problems.

- Chews and toys: Safe and appropriate chews and toys can cost more than you might realize.
- Grooming products and equipment
- Nutritious, high quality food: Nutritious food of a high quality is a non-negotiable for a healthy pet.
- High quality dog beds and/or crates
- Collars and leashes: You will have to buy several collars and leashes as your dog grows.
- Microchipping
- Licensing
- Vaccinations

Golden Retriever owners must be prepared to find fur on their furniture. This breed sheds its undercoat heavily in the spring and fall, and there is continual shedding all through the year. You will need to brush your Golden Retriever on a regular basis.

Like many other dogs, Golden Retrievers also often take on an unpleasant "dog smell". This is something that you will have to get used to. It will be necessary to bathe your Golden Retriever on occasion.

Prospective Golden Retriever owners must be extremely social and affectionate with their dogs. A

Golden Retriever will become upset and depressed if it thinks its owner does not want to be around it on an extremely frequent basis.

As a result, Golden Retrievers are not generally a suitable breed for people who work very long hours.

As with any dog, you must be willing to put in the time necessary to properly train and socialize your dog. Don't assume that that the Golden Retriever's naturally sweet nature means that training isn't necessary: that is a major mistake!

You should be aware that Golden Retrievers tend to be prone to a number of medical conditions that can be both distressing and expensive to deal with. They have a higher rate of cancer than the majority of other dog breeds.

Your commitment to being a devoted dog owner is necessary to the happiness, health, and proper training of your pet. Dogs adopted by people lacking the necessary dedication and commitment all too often end up in rescues.

Getting a puppy is never something that should be done impulsively. You should think about the question for a significant amount of time, weighing all considerations.

You should consider getting a dog only if you have discussed it at length with your family, and all members of your household have said that they would like to have a dog.

If you get a dog against your family's wishes, your dog might develop psychological problems because of your family's unwillingness to pay attention to it and interact with it.

How Does a Golden Retriever Differ from a Labrador Retriever?

Many people get confused between the Golden Retriever and Labrador Retriever, even imagining that they are somehow the same breed. This is not the case.

While they do have many similarities, The Golden Retriever and Labrador Retriever are two distinct breeds with a variety of different characteristics.

Golden Retrievers require more grooming than Labrador Retrievers. This is because of its long, thick coat. The Golden Retriever's coat can be either flat or wavy with a distinct "smiling" facial expression, as well as a longer snout.

They are less muscular in build than Labrador Retrievers, and usually slightly lighter in weight. While the average weight of a Golden Retriever is between 55 and 75 pounds, that of a Labrador Retriever is between 65 and 80.

What Kinds of Exercise Do Golden Retrievers Like Best?

Golden Retrievers enjoy a wide range of exercise activities. Some of these are:

- Walking and running: Your Golden Retriever will need lots of walks as well as opportunities to run. If you jog, take your Golden Retriever with you.
- Jumping: You can find ways to encourage your dog to jump both outdoors and indoors.
- Playing hide and seek: Your Golden Retriever will love a game of hide and seek with his human companion.
- Tug of war: Get a special tug-of-war rope toy for dogs from a pet store. Most Golden Retrievers enjoy this game and play it in a good-natured way. However, the game might encourage aggressive or even predatory behavior in some dogs (yes, even Golden Retrievers). If you notice this, avoid this game.

- Hiding treats: Hiding treats and encouraging your dog to find them is a fun game for Golden Retrievers.
- Chasing a laser pointer: Believe it not, your Golden Retriever might enjoy chasing a laser pointer! Be careful never to accidentally shine the laser pointer in the dog's eyes, as it can cause damage to the retina.
- Dock diving: If your Golden Retriever adores water (which he likely will) and once he is an experienced swimmer, you could consider dock diving.

Dock diving combines diving, swimming, and the game of fetch. Simply throw one of your dog's floating toys into the water. He will swim to

retrieve it and bring it back to you. You can repeat this process again and again. Make sure that you do not do dock diving in places that potentially have hidden objects (such as rocks) in the water that could pose a danger to your dog.
- Walking or running on a treadmill: In addition to walking and running outside (which your dog also needs), walking or running on a treadmill can be fun for dogs who are able to learn how to use it safely. This can be a good option for extra exercise during the cold winter months.
- Swimming: Most Golden Retrievers love the water. This is because they were bred to retrieve birds from the water, for hunters. Keep a close eye on your Golden Retriever as they first learn to swim.
- Agility training: Agility training is a great choice of activity for Golden Retrievers. It will help keep your pet physically and mentally occupied, and burn off lots of energy!
- Hiking: Hiking can be a wonderful activity for Golden Retrievers as long as they are not too

old or otherwise not fit for the task. Hiking isn't usually appropriate for puppies. Adult dogs will like this activity best. Make sure to consult with your vet before undertaking a long hike.
- Fetch: Play fetch with your dog on a regular basis. Golden Retrievers are some of the biggest fans of this popular game.

Walking

Several daily walks are a must for any breed of large dog, and Golden Retrievers are certainly no exception. These walks are necessary to keep your Golden Retriever happy and healthy, and to help ensure that he or she will be happy and healthy when they reach old age.

Going for walks is not only an excellent chance for bonding with your dog, but is also an adventure that will give your dog much needed physical and mental stimulation. This stimulation is essential for the well-being of your dog.

Remember that the Golden Retriever is a sporting and hunting dog, and loves to investigate and see new things. It is important to remember that even though the dog is a hunting dog, you should never allow it to run after and potentially hurt small animals.

Remember that Golden Retrievers are an excellent dog for jogging with. Always keep your dog's age in mind, though. You should never push your dog past what he or she can do without strain. Talk to your vet if you are uncertain on this point.

Hunting

As we discussed earlier, you should never allow your dog to run after or hunt small animals. Let your dog use his hunting instincts for happier pursuits. Remember what we said earlier about the fun games of hide and seek and hunting for treats.

Your dog might also enjoy the challenge of food puzzles. Food puzzles are special containers that make your dog think in order to get access to his food. You can find food puzzles at pet food stores. Make sure to do research to ensure that you get a food puzzle that is appropriate for your pet.

Playtime

Your Golden Retriever needs lots of playtime. Set aside an ample amount of time for play each and every day. This will be bonding time as well as much needed exercise time for your pet.

We discussed a variety of types of play that Golden Retrievers tend to enjoy earlier on in this e-book. Some examples include fetch, dock diving, hiding treats, tug of war, and hide and seek. Make sure to refer back to that section for details.

Choosing a Golden Retriever Puppy

Have you decided that a Golden Retriever puppy is the right choice for you? If after carefully considering the question you decide that getting a Golden Retriever is a good decision for both you and the dog, you need to find a reputable breeder.

Don't underestimate how important it is to find a good and reputable breeder. Getting a puppy from a breeder that is less reputable puts you at risk of getting a dog that has serious genetic problems.

It also supports people who often mistreat and abuse dogs (like puppy mill owners). Ensure that the breeder you choose is able to give you complete information on the puppy's full family lineage, and its registration papers.

Choosing a reputable breeder means that you will not end up with an inbred puppy. Remember that inbreeding very often leads to medical problems that will cause suffering for the dog as well as expensive vet bills.

Having your dog's family lineage and registration papers will probably give you a sense of what your dog will be as an adult: its eventual size, coat length and texture, coloring, and general temperament.

Some medical and psychological conditions are hereditary, so knowing your dog's lineage might help to prevent your ending up with a puppy with a worrying condition.

Your dog's linage will set out information on his or her mother (dam) and sire (father), and any conditions his or her dam and sire or ancestors going further back suffered from. Examples of potential issues might include joint dysplasia, arthritis, cardiovascular issues, and gastric dilation).

Remember that your cuddly Golden Retriever puppy will grow up quickly and will one day be a large and energetic dog. You need to begin training your puppy properly from the beginning. Failing to do so will only cause headaches in the future. The failure to properly train puppies is one of the most common reasons why dogs eventually end up in shelters.

You should begin basic training with your Golden Retriever puppy from when you first get it home. This helps to avoid the formation of any lasting bad habits. Puppies are far more intelligent than most people give them credit for, and this is especially the case with highly intelligent dogs like Golden Retrievers (which, as we mentioned earlier, is the fourth most intelligent breed of dog).

They are able to learn simple commands much more rapidly than you likely imagine. You need for your puppy to learn the rules of your family (or the "pack"), as soon as possible.

Golden Retrievers are loyal pets and love their human companions. This means that praise is a very effective reward in training. You will find that your dog's respect for you will continue to development as you teach, train and discipline him.

You will soon find that your puppy will follow commands because he knows that you will be pleased, and your being pleased is a very great reward to him.

Your dog cannot be expected to know and understand his or her position in your family if you fail to train him or her properly. It needs to be clear form the beginning that you are the pack leader and therefore in charge of the household as a whole and everything that happens within it (this includes outside your house, too).

What to Do After You've Brought Your Golden Retriever Puppy Home

Remember that your new puppy has just been taken away from its mother and siblings. This is always extremely difficult, and no matter how much love or reassurance you give it, your puppy will be nervous and scared at first. He is in a new pack, and does not yet know your family and its new environment.

Your puppy will likely feel very lonely at first, and this means that you have to spend a great deal of time interacting with him. Dogs are good at hiding their emotions sometimes, so don't assume that he is not lonely just because he seems playful and frisky.

Comfort the puppy by giving him things like a stuffed toy and soft, warm bed. The stuffed toy should be a little larger than the puppy. This will help him feel comforted. He will cuddle up to it and feel comforted and soothed in the absence of his mother and siblings. Your puppy should be able to keep his stuffed toy for as long as he likes.

Your puppy's "potty" or "bathroom" training should begin very early on. This means that you need to gently let the puppy be aware of where it is and the fact that it isn't acceptable to go relieve itself inside.

You will need to have a lot of patience when doing potty training. Some puppies become confused and need time to learn. Be kind and consistent. Never show impatience.

You should never allow or encourage your puppy to bite or jump on people or the furniture, even when it is very young and small. Remember that you do not want bad habits to develop that could continue into adulthood when your dog will be much larger and stronger.

Make sure that your puppy has its own toys and bedding. It should know from the beginning that these are the things that belong to him, and that he should not interfere with the human's possessions.

This will be very effective in preventing the dog from chewing up your possessions later on. A good rule of thumb is to never let your puppy continue in doing things that you would find objectionable in an adult dog.

Communicating with Your Golden Retriever

In order to communicate effectively with your Golden Retriever, you have to speak in a language that your dog can understand. Effective communication is necessary because it is necessary for proper bonding and training.

One of your most effective tools in communicating with your dog is that of tone of voice. Another is body positioning and body language. Your dog is extremely sensitive to these elements of communication, more so than to the actual words that are said. This makes sense, as when dogs or wolves communicate and relate to one another, it is tone and body language that sends the desired message.

You will find that your dog has a variety of barks and other sounds, and that each has its own general tone. He or she will likely have greeting noises, happy barks, whines, whimpers, attention seeking sounds, and playful barks.

Always ensue that the tone you use when talking to your dog precisely matches the sentiment or emotion that you want your dog to understand you to be expressing.

An example of this would be using a happy, upbeat, preferably high-pitched voice when giving praise for behavior you would like your dog to continue with. You should use a sign of affection, such as a pat or little treat, to help reinforce this message.

It is important that you never shout or yell at your pet dog. Dogs do not understand the motivation behind yelling or shouting. They will see it only as aggression rather than any sort of reprimand. As your dog will think that you are being aggressive with him, he might become nervous and frightened.

The best thing to do instead of this is to make a little, low-toned growl similar to that a mother dog would do. A good way to approximating this is to use a short, low-toned reprimand. One example is "ah, ah", using a low, sharp voice. Dogs usually understand that you are reprimanding them when you do this.

Many people make the mistake of accidentally rewarding your Golden Retriever for behavior that is either bad or negative in some other way. If your dog is frightened of something and you use a tone of voice that you think to be reassuring, he or she might think that you are praising them for being nervous and that he or she should be nervous again in similar situations.

Only give your Golden Retriever treats when he does something that you would like him to do again. This is important, because if you give some treats for no reason on a consistent basis, they will lose their efficacy as a reward in the dog's mind.

This means that treats will no longer be an effective way of rewarding your dog for being obedient, causing problems in training.

Remember that if a reward is given, it should be done *after* the dog has done something that you wanted him to do. It should never be given as a bribe, which means before the dog has done what it should do.

Disciplining Your Dog

If you're like many people, you probably have a mistaken view of what disciplining your dog is or should be. Yelling and smacking are never thing that you should resort to. Not only are they ineffective, they could make your dog develop psychological problems.

Yelling or smacking could lead to your Golden Retriever becoming depressed, confused, fearful, or nervous, and it is very likely that the undesirable behavior could worsen. Remember that dogs always see yelling and hitting as aggression, and what's worse, as aggression that isn't in any way justified. This will create serious trust issues between you and your dog.

You need to ensure that you use communication that your dog can understand when you discipline him. If your dog is unable to understand the message you seek to communicate, how can your discipline be effective?

The answer is simple: it cannot. Discipline needs to use effective communication, and it must lead to your dog's understanding that you are leader of the household and the "pack". One reason for this is the fact that dogs are always keen to make their leader pleased with their behavior.

Just turning away and ignoring your dog with your arms folded when he does something bad is a very effective reprimand. He wants to please you, and your showing that you are anything but pleased will make him want to change his behavior. The dog will be unlikely to repeat the behavior.

Give your dog lots of praise and affection and use a high-pitched, cheerful tone of voice when your dog exhibits good behavior. It is essential that you do this immediately, as this will ensure that the reward is properly connected to your dog's behavior in his mind.

You need to make your dog understand how he can earn and maintain your approval and praise. This is an extremely effective tool in discipline.

Potty Training Your Puppy

A great deal of patience is always essential in potty training your puppy. You will have to understand and remember that puppies tend to become a bit confused during the potty-training process. It is your responsibility as a caring and knowledgeable dog owner to be patient and consistent and give your dog the time they require to learn.

Maybe you're wondering why it is that puppies tend to become confused during toilet training. In order to understand, you have to think about it from the dog's perspective.

When toilet training, you need to praise your puppy the first time he relieves himself outside. He may be a bit confused by this, wondering why you are praising him for going to the bathroom. He will probably not immediately connect this with the idea of going to the bathroom *outside*.

It is because of this potential misunderstanding that you might find that your puppy comes up to you inside and relieves himself in front of you, thinking he's making you happy and expecting praise. If you see your puppy doing this or getting ready to do this, simply do this: silently pick him up and bring him outside.

Do not say anything, and do not show any sign of anger. Once the dog is outside, say "go pee" or "go potty" to encourage the puppy to relieve himself. After the dog has gone to the bathroom outside, give him the reward of praise and patting.

Clean up the mess the puppy made inside as soon as you get indoors. Do this silently, and do not make eye contact with the dog. Do not reprimand the dog in any way, and do not show any sort of impatience or anger.

After doing this process several times, you will discover that your puppy will seek to get your attention when he needs to go outdoors to go to the potty.

Make sure that you bring your puppy outside so he can go to the bathroom when he wakes up in the morning, when he wakes up from naps, after each meal, and just before he goes to bed at night.

Basic Obedience Training

Golden Retrievers are not only docile and friendly but highly intelligent and cooperative, as well. They are known for being a cooperative breed that is easy to train. They have a sensible and calm disposition and are reliable with a strong work ethic.

They are always eager to please their human companions. This means that training a Golden Retriever is often easier than dealing with many other breeds.

With any breed of dog, however, it is always essential to know what you are doing and always take the right approach. You must always communicate with your dog in a way that your dog will understand.

Patience and calm is needed at all times in order for your dog to be responsive and your training to be effective.

If you notice that any miscommunications take place, do what you can to remedy them immediately.

Effective training always requires a positive reward system. When your Golden Retriever behaves in the way you want him to and practices good behavior, you need to give him a reward to reinforce the behavior.

To help in the process of teaching your dog commands, say each command when your dog is doing the corresponding action. This will help your dog quickly learn what each command means. An example of this in practice would be saying the command "Sit" when you see your dog sit.

Remember: never give up in your efforts. It is essential that you be consistent and persistent in your training of your puppy. Failing to do this means that your dog could quickly and easily become confused, and interfere with any future training.

Know Your Dog

Focus on getting to know your dog as an individual. Many people do not realize that dogs can vary in their napping and general sleep patterns. Different dogs will have their own unique times of the day in which they are most energetic and inclined to be attentive and active.

You would be well-advised to do training when he is most energetic. If your dog tends to take naps in the afternoon, it would be best to schedule training in the morning and/or following the puppy's afternoon nap.

Quickly Get Your Dog Accustomed to his Name

Start getting your puppy accustomed to his name from the very beginning, saying it as often as possible. It is especially important to do this when trying to get his attention.

Make a point of calling the dog by name when you are about to feed him. This is also important when you want to take him for a walk and when you want to play with him.

Watch Out for Signs that Your Dog Might Not Trust You

A sign of a dog's lack of trust in its owner is often leaning away when the owner attempts to reach for it. If you notice your dog doing this, you will need to work on building up the trust in your relationship with your pet.

There are many things that you can do to help build your dog's trust in you. These include:

- Trying to see and understand the world the way your dog does, through canine eyes.
- Always being your pet's protector. Let your dog know that you would never put him in a dangerous situation.
- Spending more quality time with your dog.
- Always being fair and consistent. It's essential that your dog has a dependable owner and predictable environment.
- Being invariably affectionate and kind.

Below are signs that you have a strong bond with your dog:

- Your dog clearly loves physical interaction with you.
- Your dog seems to keep track of where you are at all times, when he or she is off the leash.
- Your dog would be willing to provide you with help or protection if you were in danger.
- Your dog does not show any hesitation when you ask him or her to obey.
- Your dog is able to communicate its concerns, needs, and wants to you.
- Your dog clearly loves being near you.
- Your dog adjusts his or her pace to suit yours, when walking.
- Your dog looks at you frequently, showing his or her focus on you.
- Your dog comes to you when you call him or her, even in situations where there are distractions (this is a particularly challenging task for many dogs).

There are many things that you can do to develop a stronger bond with your dog. Some of these include:

- Petting and grooming your dog on a regular basis.
- Teaching your dog new tricks regularly.
- Choosing specific times of the day at which to always feed your dog.
- Playing hide and seek with your dog. This will help your dog see being with you as a reward.
- Using the "come" (recall) command more often.
- Doing more playtime activities with your dog.

How to Teach Your Golden Retriever to Sit on Command

Teaching your Golden Retriever to sit will probably be a relatively easy process. To teach your dog how to sit on command, hold a treat close to and a little bit above your Golden Retriever's dog.

You will find that your dog will try to tilt its head back. He will continue to do so, trying to reach the treat, until he eventually ends up sitting accidentally. When you see that he is sitting, say "sit".

Reward your dog with the treat and give him lots of praise, making sure to say "good dog!" You should give him affection too, with patting.

With this process, your Golden Retriever will quickly learn that "sit" means he needs to get into the sitting position. He will also know that when he sits, he gets affection and treats.

How to Teach Your Golden Retriever to Drop on Command

Teaching a dog to drop is generally one of the easiest commands to teach. The "drop" command tells a dog to lie down on its belly. Your dog needs to know the "sit" command before he can learn the "drop" one.

The first step in the process of teaching the drop command is to hold a treat above your Golden Retriever's nose. Say "sit".

Once your dog sits, adjust the position of the treat down, moving it towards your dog's front feet. After that, move is very slightly forward.

You will find that your dog will lower the position of its head, trying to get the treat. Once you see this, gently nudge your Golden Retriever's shoulders to encourage him into a prone position.

Once your dog is lying down in the correct way, say "drop". Give him the treat. You should do this about twice a day until your dog drops on command.

How to Teach Your Golden Retriever to Come on Command (Recall)

No matter whether or not you plan to ever bring your Golden Retriever somewhere where he'll be off the leash and you will have to call him back to you, it is important that you train your dog to come back on command (recall).

In order to train your Golden Retrieval to come on command, you need to associate coming back to you with positive things.

Your dog will not come back to you if he thinks that you are hostile or angry at him for any reason. The first thing you need to know to do this training is to bring your dog to a park, on a very long leash.

Make sure that you still maintain control while letting him roam around on the long leash. Once a few minutes have gone by, he will have stopped focussing on you.

Use a high-pitched and enthusiastic tone to say the command "come". You must be standing especially upright as you do this, and hold open your arms as if you are asking for a hug. Give your dog praise and a treat when he comes to you.

If your dog does not come to you, say the command again and tug at the leash gently. You will need to continue doing this until the dog obeys. When he comes to you, tell him to "sit" and the give him a treat.

Keep carrying out this process every time you go for a walk. Remember to gradually make the distance you let him roam longer and longer before you use the "come" command.

How to Teach Your Golden Retriever to Fetch on Command

It surprises some new dog owners to find out that not all dogs necessarily know how to play fetch automatically. It is true, though, that as retrievers, Golden Retrievers do tend to be good at this game from the start. Fetch is a fun game that you and your dog will enjoy.

Most people use a tennis ball for playing fetch with their dogs. This is a generally good choice, as it is easy for a dog to properly grip with their teeth and it's an appropriate size.

If you find that you need to train your dog how to play fetch, first roll the tennis ball across the ground. Encourage your Golden Retriever to chase it, using an enthusiastic tone of voice.

After your dog retrieves the ball, make sure to say "fetch". This is how your dog will learn the fetch command.

Reward the dog with praise and petting once he has picked up the ball. He will now know that when he picks up a ball that you have rolled, he will be rewarded. This will make him always pick it up.

After your dog has practiced this a few times, do not give him the treat after he picks up the ball but rather wait for him to bring it back to you.

It's at that point that you can give him the treat and praise. You should do this a number of times. Your dog will soon know what "fetch" means and how to play the game.

How to Teach Your Golden Retriever to Stay on Command

You need to teach your Golden Retriever to stay when you give him the "stay" command. This is a necessary command in a wide variety of circumstances. Some of these can include when you have need your dog to stay away from the front door when you are opening it for a visitor, when you need to train your dog to not begin eating out of its bowl until you have given permission, and when you need to stop your dog from getting out of the yard.

Hold a treat over your Golden Retriever's nose and use the "sit" command. Once your dog sits, surprise him by not giving him the expected treat and have him in suspense for a few moments.

Then, use a confident and firm tone of voice to say "stay". After that, hold up one of your hands.

Make the palm face outwards with the fingers together. With your hand held like this, step away from your pet. After one step, again say the "stay" command.

Wait a few seconds, and then say the command "stay" again. Step towards the dog. If your pet has followed the command as you wished until you got to him, give him the treat and praise. You will need to practice this on a regular basis.

You will risk ruining this training if you ever call your dog after telling him to stay. This will confuse him and make it difficult for him to understand what you want him to do the next time you say stay.

Every time you tell your dog to stay, it is imperative that he only start moving once you have returned to where he is.

How to Teach Your Golden Retriever to Wait on Command

Some new dog owners do not realize this, but "stay" and "wait" are two entirely different commands. While with the "stay" command, the dog is released from the command when you go back to him, with the "wait" command, your dog is required to stay where he is only until you call to him so that he comes to you. This is a vital distinction that you must always remember if you are not to confuse your dog and undo your training efforts.

Since so many dog owners can get a bit confused about the difference between these two commands, it's really no wonder that many dogs will need a bit of time to understand it.

You will need to be patient. As long as you are consistent and persistent, your dog will come to understand these essential commands.

You might be wondering in what kinds of situations that the wait command is useful. One is when you are crossing a street with your Golden Retriever. You will need your dog to wait without any objection until you deem crossing to be safe.

This is the kind of circumstance in which the wait command is indispensable. It will prevent your dog tugging at the leash and potentially putting himself (and perhaps you) in a dangerous situation.

Your enunciation of the wait command does not need to be quite as sharp as with stay. It does need to be firm, however.

To teach your Golden Retriever to understand and follow the wait command, have your dog sit and then say "wait". This should be in a tone that is firm but not quite as sharp as the stay command. Once you have done this, move a little bit away from your pet, and then call him over to you.

Leash Training Your Golden Retriever

It is essential that every dog know how to properly walk on a leash. This is necessary for a number of reasons. If you're like most of us, you have probably seen someone being dragged by their dog on a leash on a sidewalk or in the park. This situation makes it difficult for the pet owner to give their dog the exercise and recreation it needs.

One of the most important points to remember is that dogs should never pull their human companions around. Dogs who do this have not been given proper training, and therefore fail to understand that their owner is the pack leader. It is pulling its owner around because it imagines that it is leading the "hunt".

The Golden Retriever is a dog that is relatively substantial in size, and this makes it even more important than it might be otherwise that it is properly leash trained. Even though the Golden Retriever tends to be a docile and sweet-natured breed, it is quite strong as an adult and needs proper training as a puppy.

Effective leash training must begin quite early in the dog's life. It is essential that your Golden Retriever learn what it means to "heel". When your dog is told to heel, he or she must position his nose immediately beside your left knee.

During the first stages of leash training and when you and your dog are having your first walks outside, your Golden Retriever ought to always be at heel. Once your dog has more practice of walking on a leash, you will be able to allow him to stand at a slightly further distance and sniff more of the ground, examining his environment. The default position needs to be a heel, though, and your dog must understand this.

Selecting the Right Leash and Collar

The collar you choose for your Golden Retriever must fit the dog properly. Be aware that you will need to purchase several quality collars over the course of your pet's life, as your dog will grow and change size. This will especially be the case in your dog's first couple of years of life.

You will have to buy a new collar every time the size of your dog's neck changes. Training always goes much more smoothly when the dog's collar fits as it should.

Leash Training Your Golden Retriever Puppy

The Golden Retriever's high level of intelligence combined with its cooperative nature and eagerness to please means that it tends to be easier than many other breeds to leash train.

You might find that your dog does not need the same amount of time as other dogs to get used to the feeling of having a collar on and being led on a leash. You will probably discover that it takes your Golden Retriever very little time to understand what it means to have on a leash.

For your puppy's first walk, take him or her on a very short one just in your front yard or at the most a tiny bit down the street (for example, one or two houses away from your place of residence). The main goals of the first walk will be to make your dog understand that there is no danger involved in going for a walk and therefore no need for alarm, and to get him used to walking on a leash.

Any puppy will experience a bit of confusion when you first start leash training, and you will need to give your Golden Retriever some gentle encouragement. This will help him feel safe and confident in trusting you.

You will probably find that your puppy is a bit uncertain as to what he is supposed to do at first. When this happens, you will have to fall back a step or two and turn to encourage him. Your tone of voice should be cheerful.

It is imperative that you never end up dragging your puppy, as doing so could traumatize your dog and make it associate going for walks with feelings of ear and uncertainty.

Similarly, you ought to never jerk your dog back with the leash when it runs forward in front of you. Instead, use a cheerful tone of voice to call him back. Jerking the leash will cause your puppy to feel nervous and scared of going for walks.

Your puppy's first walk on a leash should be very short. It is important that your puppy sees walks as exciting and fun adventures with its human companion that it should look forward to.

Next Steps in Leash Training

It may take a while for your dog to really understand that you are the definitive leader of the pack and always will be. Going for walks can be very exciting, and as your Golden Retriever grows in confidence he might try to test whether perhaps he could be leader of the pack instead of you.

You will have to be firm and fair at all times. In order to ensure a harmonious relationship between you and your pet, your dog must eventually realize that you are the leader and that's not going to change and what is more, he is happy about that!

You will probably find that your Golden Retriever tries to pull ahead of you on occasion, to test your response. At this point, you will have the duty to be firm and enforce the rules that you have taught your dog. To do so, you will need to use some additional training techniques.

If your dog pulls ahead of you, simply turn sharply and walk in the opposite direction. There is no reason to raise your voice or show any kind of anger to your dog; you should be aware that doing so might actually make the situation worse.

Use a high-pitched, cheerful tone as you do this, and enunciate the word "watching". This is a new command that your dog will learn means that you are turning around to the opposite direction and thwarting the walk as a result of his behavior.

The "watching" command tells your dog that he is required to pay close attention to your actions, as you are changing your direction. If it needs to do so, it is hoped that your dog will run if necessary in order to catch up with you.

After your dog has run to catch up with you after changing direction, enunciate the "heel" command. This command orders your dog to position his head near your leg (you will remember that we explained this earlier). Give your dog praise after he has moved a few steps in this way.

You might find that your dog is slightly confused, at least at first. If so, you might find it necessary to do all of this several times until your dog is able to understand. When your Golden Retriever tries to walk ahead of you, use the "ah ah" reprimand we discussed earlier, using a low, almost growly, and sharp tone of voice. Once you have done that, turn in the opposite direction while saying "watching" cheerfully.

At this point, your dog should run to catch up with you. When he has reached you, say "heel" to bring your dog to heel and give him praise. The longer your dog remains at heel, the more praise you should bestow on him.

What to Do When Coming Across Strangers and Other Dogs

It is a certainty that as you go for walks outside with your dog, you will encounter strangers and other dogs. Individual dogs differ in their reactions to such experiences. When your dog is approached by another dog, you may find that they have a positive reaction and eagerly greet what he sees to be a new friend, or he might growl and be aggressive and fearful.

Signs of aggression and fearfulness might include your dog raising his hackles, thus making himself appear menacing, and/or growling. This sort of body language and vocalization is meant as a warning to prevent unknown people or dogs coming any closer.

Regardless of what your dog's initial reaction may be, it's crucial that he learns that there is nothing to fear when encountering other dogs and/or new people. He will also learn the equally important fact that it is never acceptable to suddenly run over to people or dogs. Many dogs and people alike might be alarmed at the sight of a strange dog rushing towards them.

Get your dog to sit down if he appears nervous when another dog or a stranger is coming near. When you do so, lavish him with praise as the dog or stranger approaches, and do what you can to make him feel reassured and calm. Talk to him in a cheerful voice as you let him know that everything will be okay.

Doing all of these things in a conscientious way will make your dog quickly recognize that there is no reason for him to be fearful or nervous in these situations. Your dog will know that there is no reason for him to try to protect you from other dogs or strangers, and that there is no threat of any kind to be concerned about.

Socializing Your Golden Retriever

Golden Retrievers are prized for their cooperative and loyal temperaments. They love to be with their owners and families, and are more easily and quickly socialized than many other breeds. They love nothing more than pleasing their human companions.

While all of this is true, it is important never to forget that all dogs, even Golden Retrievers, require socialization in order to live happily with humans and deal with everything and everyone they will come across in their lives as domestic pets. You need to ensure that your dog will never think it is necessary to be aggressive or fearful.

It is quite common for people to think that socializing a dog means that you must have the dog play with other dogs, for example, in a dog park, or make playdates with dogs belonging to neighbors.

This is not true. Some dogs do not respond to this in a positive way, although, as Golden Retrievers are such a friendly breed, it is quite likely that your dog would indeed enjoy this. A Golden Retriever will be more likely to enjoy playing with dogs from "other packs" than many other, more territorial breeds (such as the German Shepherd).

So, socializing your dog does not necessarily mean that you have to arrange for him to play with other dogs; rather it requires you to teach him the appropriate ways to react in situations where he comes across unknown people or other dogs (in other words, members of other or perhaps even rival "packs").

One excellent step you can take in this process is to arrange for your puppy to participate in a puppy class. Doing so will help to make sure that your Golden Retriever learns the proper ways to interact with other dogs while he is still very young.

Having this experience when still a very young puppy will make positive reactions in uncertain situations automatic when your pet becomes an adult dog.

How to Address Your Dog's Chewing or Biting

Every dog owner needs to understand that canines need to chew. There is nothing you can do to stop it, and you should not want to, as chewing is necessary for the proper development and eventual strength of the dog's jaws.

It will be your goal to conscientiously teach your Golden Retriever that he cannot chew on your possessions but should do so with his own special chew toys. This might sound easy, but it will probably take a good deal of patience and dedication.

You need to direct your dog's need and desire to chew in the right way. You should never try to stop your dog from chewing. It is a necessary activity for the animal's physical and psychological well-being and development.

If you catch your Golden Retriever chewing on one of your possession or something else that you do not want the dog to chew on, the first thing you should do is to simply take the item away from him. Keep completely silent as you do this, and never give any impression of reprimand or scolding. Give your pet one of his own chew toys and encourage him to chew on that. Give your Golden Retriever lots of praise when you see him chewing on his own toy.

Look for chew toys that are non-toxic and specifically made for dogs. You should keep a good supply of these at all times. You will need to do research to make sure that the toys you buy are indeed safe for your dogs to chew.

They cannot have any appendages that may come loose and be accidentally swallowed by your dog. This could cause choking and cause damage to the stomach or throat.

Be patient with your dog, allowing him the time he needs to learn. Be prepared for it to possibly take longer than you would like to finally train your dog in this area. Don't give up. It is certain that eventually your dog will not be tempted to chew on any of your things, and will only wish to chew on his own chew toys.

Perhaps you have noticed that playing puppies sometimes bite one another. This type of behavior is just a form of play and the puppies do not mean one another any harm. However, it is important to train puppies out of the biting habit so that they do not continue with it when they are grown dogs and much larger and more powerful.

Some Golden Retrievers have a tendency to "mouth". When a dog "mouths", it uses its mouth to imitate the movement of a bite without any use of the teeth. They do this for two reasons, amusement and attention. Unfortunately, other dogs and people might easily find this threatening, especially when the dog doing it is relatively large (as the Golden Retriever is).

You will be pleased to hear that your dog's use of chew toys will be helpful in making your dog cease with his mouthing and play biting behaviors. Provide an immediate reprimand with a sharp "ah ah" whenever you see your pet mouthing or biting, and remove his mouth from the object of his behavior.

Once you have done that, it is essential that you immediately provide the dog with one of his chew toys. Do not say anything when doing this. Praise the dog as soon as he begins to chew on his toy.

Advanced Techniques and Agility Training

After you have successfully taught your Golden Retriever all of the basic commands, including sit, stay, wait, come, drop, and go right and left, you will be able to do more advanced training.

There are many different forms of advanced training. One of these is agility training. You might enjoy having your dog undergo training on an agility training course. Many dogs find this to be a fun challenge, and it will give your dog lots of exercise.

Agility training will require your dog to learn and make his way through agility courses (special obstacle courses). After your Golden Retriever becomes proficient at it, you could even consider putting him in competitions. Golden Retrievers are known for being an especially good breed for agility training, and do well in competitions.

If it would be impractical or perhaps impossible for you to have your dog undergo formal agility training, you could set up your own obstacle course in your backyard. Such a backyard agility course could include cones around which your dog will have to move, as well as low benches used as hurdles for jumping.

Keep in mind that your dog needs to be at least 18 months old before you can consider having him or her do any sort of agility or other advanced training.

Dogs that are younger than 18 months still have developing bones and bodies, and the injuries that can be incurred in agility training could interfere with your dog's future growth and future health.

It is indisputable that Golden Retrievers are one of the most popular dogs in agility and other types of advanced dog training. Their high level of intelligence, eagerness to please, sweet, cooperative nature, and general athleticism make them perfect for such pursuits.

Just as in basic dog training, advanced training involves using positive rewards to teach and reinforce behaviors. It is useful to remember that Golden Retrievers see the affection and praise of their human companions as the most valuable reward in the world.

Advanced training is more challenging than basic training because it can be more difficult to get your dog to understand exactly what it is you want him to do. Be patient and give your dog all the time he needs. Your dog may understandably find agility courses to be rather confusing, especially at first. You will need to dedicate a significant amount of time to teaching your dog.

When you start to train your dog in doing agility courses, you will find that the first thing you will need to do is have your dog sit to one side of the course's first hurdle. Give him the "wait" command. After that, you must move to its other side. Allow your dog to see that you are holding a treat or perhaps his favorite toy. Call the dog, showing that he must jump over the hurdle in order to get to you. As the dog jumps, say "over" or "jump" in an enthusiastic tone of voice. Lavish the dog with praise.

An alternative way to train your dog to jump over a hurdle is to simply throw his favorite ball (or any ball) over it and say "fetch". When you do this, you might find that your dog frustrates your plans by running around the hurdle and not leaping over it. If he does, throw it over again. When your dog finally does jump over the hurdle, say "over" or "jump". Give your Golden Retriever a great deal of praise.

While agility training can be a lot of fun for many dogs and their owners, it is certainly not the only type of advanced training you could try. You could train your dog to do advanced tasks within your household. For example, you could train him or her to fetch the newspaper or your slippers, or do any other specific task of which a dog could be capable.

Conclusion

The Golden Retriever is one of the most popular dog breeds in the United States and around the world. It is well-loved for its many wonderful attributes, including its intelligence, sweet nature, and eagerness to please.

They are cooperative and easy to train, and are used as a working dog in many different areas. Many even consider it to be the "perfect dog".

Golden Retrievers are well-known to be one of the best choices for a family dog, and they have the playful, affectionate, and tolerant nature needed to be good with kids. Golden Retrievers are energetic dogs that need a great deal of exercise, as well as lots of space.

The fourth most intelligent breed of dog, the Golden Retriever is a wonderful companion that needs a lot of mental stimulation. Always remember that as human beings, we have an abundance of things that we use to keep ourselves occupied, such as our computers, work, televisions, and friends. Your pet, however, depends entirely on you for absolutely everything.

If you choose to make a Golden Retriever your pet, it will be your responsibility to keep your dog happy and occupied. To say that you are too busy is never an excuse for neglect. If you doubt that you will have time to ensure that your Golden Retriever is happy and healthy, then you should refrain from getting a dog.

You must spend a great deal of time with your Golden Retriever, always letting him or her know how much you trust and love him.

Golden Retrievers need to be groomed regularly. This is necessary for your dog's health and well-being. It will also make your pet feel loved, and this is very important to psychological health. It will also make him feel like the member of the family "pack" that he really is.

If you give your Golden Retriever all of the care and affection he needs, always taking into account the unique characteristics and requirements of the breed, you will be rewarded with a remarkably wonderful family pet.

Printed in Great
Britain
by Amazon